ANOTHER RUDE AWAKENING

ANOTHER RUDE
AWAKENING

Poems by Dori Appel

Cherry Grove Collections

Published by Cherry Grove Collections
P.O. Box 541106
Cincinnati, OH 45254-1106

ISBN: 9781934999233
LCCN: 2008933136

Poetry Editor: Kevin Walzer
Business Editor: Lori Jareo

Visit us on the web at www.cherry-grove.com

Acknowledgments

Grateful acknowledgment is made to the following magazines and anthologies in which a number of these poems have appeared, some in slightly different form.

Magazines: *The Beloit Poetry Journal*: "Alter Ego" and "A Dream Making Many Things Better"; *the new renaissance*: "Abridged Novel With Predictable Outcome"; *Yankee*: "A Double Life; *Chaminade Literary Review*: "First Love"; *Jefferson Public Radio Guide to the Arts*: "In the Rose Test Gardens; Portland Oregon"; *Prairie Schooner*: "My Grandmother's Education" and "Legacy"; *Seems*: "Sleepwalker-2" and "No Permanent Address"; *The Madison Review*: "Vapors"; *Umbrella*: "Horses in Dreams."

Anthologies: Papier Mache Press:"Birthday Portrait in Muted Tones" in *When I Am an Old Woman I Shall Wear Purple;* "Finally" in *If I Had a Hammer,* women's work in poetry, fiction, and photographs; "Resumé" in *If I Had My Life to Live Over.* An earlier version of "Alter Ego" was also collected in *at our core*, Papier-Mache Press, "A Double Life" was also collected in *And a Deer's Ear, Eagle's Song and Bear's Grace,* Cleis Press, and *From Here We Speak,* an anthology of Oregon Poetry, Oregon State University Press.

For Perry

For Dashka

And in memory of my father,
George Irwin Appel

CONTENTS

WAKING

Why do we agree to it?
Isn't the amoebic merging
of the dark hours better,
the easy intertwining
of our legs as we breathe
and sleep? Then we are nameless
and infinite, indifferent to

the hours slipping out from
beneath one another,
movement of hands
on the luminous clock face,
silent growth of
hair and fingernails.

When the first dawn sneaked
across night's borders,
didn't anyone shout *Thief!*
or warn of danger coming?
How slavishly we stagger
to our feet
when daylight calls us,

our truant dreams dissolving,
blankets sighing their sad release.

I.

FRAGMENTS

Today I see Mrs. St. Clair,
lit once more by the streetlight
on that steamy August night.
She is tiny, hardly taller than
I am, and embarrassed to be
seen weeping by my mother and myself.
As we pass, she buries her face
against her thin bare arm.
She is running from the basement
apartment she shares with her husband
and her four bad boys. Right there
the picture scatters, as though
reflected in a broken mirror
in which a single, unalterable image
has been assigned to every piece.
Mrs. St. Clair runs crying,
and I can see the faces of
three sons, even though they were
behind the basement door.
But her husband and the other son
are gone, kicked under the
ugly davenport with the mirror's
lost shards. All day
hodge-podge memories flash by with
missing parts, and I look and look
at hands still held in laps and
sad, reproachful eyes,
wondering, Whose are these?
What happened next?

ALTER EGO

She walks where I walk,
this nun with her great
bird headdress,
white wings fluttering,
black robes whispering at my back.
Skimming the wintry pavement,
she plants her tranquil step
where mine has been,
a ghostly echo closing in.
Hurrying, I feel the cold air shift
as her calm contralto stirs it,

her voice the same
as mine if I could sing.

AMNESIA

1. Case History

This woman's husband
bailed out years ago. One day
he was there and the next
he was gone, leaving her
to pace the floor with
hollow-sounding steps
and open closet doors a dozen
times a day, searching
for his suits. Now
he's divorced their shared past
in an accident—
it's gone without a trace.
When she visits him
for old times' sake, his bland
unrecognizing smile
cuts her to the quick.

2. The Genre

I thought it was a fiction
invented for the movies of my youth.
The victim is always a man
we suspect of the worst,
and the woman who believes in him
seems headed for a fall. She is
a girl he met in a shop
or a psychiatrist assigned to his case,
and she fills the void with love
so that each day

he is born into a new world
beautiful as pearls.

> *This is a flower, it is called a rose,*
> *this is called a kiss.*

Still,the pieces of his lost world
haunt him. He dreams of
doors leading nowhere,
of faces hiding behind trees
in a tangled wood. He wakes
in a sweat beside this
lover, interpreter, savior,
and together they dive to his mind's
dark depths, snagging memories
like wriggling fish.
The clues accumulate:
a woman's glove, a child's doll,
an overturned car with
silent, spinning wheels.

The danger is that in
finding the truth they will
lose each other,
but in the final reel
the rediscovered wife reveals
her faithless heart
and the child's death is proved
a blameless accident.
Retrieved, the past is done.

3. *Autobiography*

A man once left my closets
and bookshelves filled with objects

we had shared, but carefully removed
the imprint of himself.
For weeks I could not respond
when called by name,
could not stay seated in a chair
or read a book. When he returned
with a few odd items taken by mistake,
they no longer seemed like mine.
There were six little knives
with flowered china handles
and harmless blades, arranged
in a lacquered case. I took one out
and held it in my hand,
unable to remember where
it came from or
what I'd used it for.

A DREAM OF FLYING

Sometimes there are reversals.
Still, it's odd to find myself
a tourist among my own
possessions, sailing over
squatting chairs and scarfaced
table tops. Being a spy
in these surroundings
makes me giddy—I mean
the *ease* of it. Below,

everything goes on as usual,
mealtime conversation
clink of knives and forks.
My shadow on the ceiling
is enormous, but no one
even glances up to see me
stranded like a shipwreck's
last survivor,
hopelessly afloat.

RITUALS FOR TWO FATHERS

In my parents' house
tradition didn't stand a chance
if safety was at stake.
Instead of a candle, my mother kept
her father's *yahrzeit* with
a light bulb in her closet,
forty watts left burning while
the sun and moon kept watch
and the clock's hands circled twice.
If she said a prayer I never heard it,
so knowing none
I light my father's candle
silently, thinking of his ashes
scattered in the Arizona mountains,
and also of my mother,
pinning a note to her closet door,
 Do not turn off this light

LANYARD

1. Earlier

Until Parents Weekend at Camp Ojibwa
my mother would have said that
a lanyard was something on a ship,
and my father, who'd swallowed a
dictionary around the time he quit
high school to help his family,
might have added that it was
a short rope used to secure the
ship's rigging. Until Parents Weekend
knowing that much was enough.

2. Afternoon Sports

They arrive on a Friday afternoon,
sniffing the air like tourists
entering an exotic foreign restaurant.
It's strange to be surrounded by
such tall trees, with pine cones
crunching beneath their shoes
(low-heeled wedgies, polished wingtips),
but they're excited as they head for the
sunny ball field in the company of
other parents in city clothes,
friendly people who smile as they exchange
the names of their sons' cabins
(Chippewa, Menominee).
The game has already started,
and my parents shield their eyes
against the glare while searching
bases and infield, finally locating my brother

at the outfield's furthest boundary
(untucked jersey, gold-rimmed specs).
They wave, then call his name,
while he fiddles unaware
with something in his hands.
Has he gone blind and deaf?
When they figure out what he's doing
they're dumfounded: In the middle of
a game their son is weaving
strands of green and purple plastic
into some kind of rope!

My mother doesn't care about the game—
she scarcely knows the rudiments and
secretly hopes it will end soon,
so much noise and running and
kicking up dust. But my father
(immigrants' son, White Socks fan)
winces as he pulls out a pack
of Chesterfields and silently lights up.
This isn't some goddamned
sandlot game, it's Afternoon Sports
at the kind of expensive private camp
he never knew existed as a kid
(ten hour workdays, stifling heat.)

The lanyard's shiny filaments
gleam in the sunlight as my brother
plaits them, his lowered forehead
damp and his shoulders hunched as
those of any sweatshop grunt.
When a ball flies close to where
he's standing, he misses it, his face
like someone waking from a dream.

But the spell is broken. He remembers
Parents Weekend, finds their two
familiar faces in the crowd,
and waves while they wave back,
the cigarette in my father's hand
smudging the air with smoke.

3. Later the Same Day

After the game, my parents
give him the tin of homemade
cookies they'd stashed in
the shade of the Director's office
(oatmeal raisin, chocolate chip),
and he gives them the finished lanyard,
plus another he made last week.
My mother's is for holding the key
to the laundry basement and
my father's, which is blue and silver,
sports a whistle for calling the collie
my brother dreams about.

A DOUBLE LIFE

A girl who loved horses thought
she was a horse. Her brown shoes
that laced were her hooves,
her neck, not long, became long
when she thought about who she was.
She told no one. When they called
her for supper she came at an
obedient trot and tucked her napkin
just above the place where
the martingale had left its mark.
When they took her places she walked
properly and answered courteously,
and thought about the sweet grass
in the field where she greeted
the morning, and the moonlight in
the meadow where she ran at night.
The morning was gold and
the night was silver, and only she
in all the world was awake to its
secret sounds and shadows,
her hooves bright as stars, her
long neck arcing towards the moon.

BEFORE AND AFTER

What was she besides beautiful?
The question had no meaning
until a man they hardly knew
shouted *mazel tov!*
and threw his glass.
Then the whole noisy crowd
echoed *mazel tov!,*
blew their noisemakers,
kissed each other—
> *Happy New Year!*
> *Happy New Year!*
> *Mazel tov!*
while my Aunt Estelle
tried too late
to shield her face.

(The eye was replaced
with a false one that
neither saw nor moved,
but filled the empty space.)

The next things to go
were her breasts,
first one, then the other.
At my uncle's insistence,
her doctors never uttered
the C word, but spoke of
"preventative measures"
with such certainty
that she never asked
exactly what that meant.

All she had left then
was her life,
which she surrendered
without much fuss—
this sweet-tempered woman
who was beautiful
in a time when that
ought to have been enough.

VAPORS

Aunt Lillian had them,
terrifying everyone so completely
that a wire was sent to Uncle Vilmesh
by expensive trans-Atlantic cable.
All right, it said, *come back*.

When I was a child
she had been widowed many years,
but she was vaporous still.
Her pale eyes were hazy behind
her rimless glasses,
her face a milky veil above
the collars of her dark
crepe dresses and pearls.
Her skin was beautiful and famous,
but not the reliable windbreaker
skin should be. Aunt Lillian looked
as though she could just dissipate,
her soft white hair still clinging
to her head by its perm while
her body escaped confining clothes
like a ghost dissolving into mists.

By that time she was
a Christian Scientist,
disbelieving the body's ills
 (a goiter scar hidden beneath
her pearls). Calm as a pudding,
she ate dreamily when she came
to dinner, while I quarreled
with my brother at the table and

our parents scolded,
and I cried into my plate.

Was this possibly the same woman
who, by the strange force of
her ethereal distress
succeeded in bringing to the altar
her father's brother Vilmesh?
Oh no, they hastened to explain,
not exactly that, though they had
the same father, because
the first mother died, poor thing,
and there was another one.
(The boys had shared a room,
 perhaps a bed, but not a womb.)
And mild Aunt Lillian
at the age of eighteen said,
"I will have him!"
and threatened to evaporate.

The facts were never mentioned
outside the family,
although my mother insisted
they would not cause
lifted brows in Europe
where villages were small
and blood was intermixed as easily
as new wine poured into the barrel
where the old had been.
Uncle Vilmesh died gracefully
and young, their one son
left no progeny,
and Aunt Lillian at eighty-four

drifted without fanfare
into the mackerel sky.

"She had the vapors,"
my mother now recalls.
"She just kept throwing up
until the doctor said,
'You'd better call him back.'"

For a moment the phone wire
tingles with wild excitement
and light bulbs explode
dizzying gases in my head.
"Pregnant!" I gasp, before
she can throw her skirts
over the bloated word. At my ear
the wire hums like Gypsy strings
gone mad as my mother's voice
grows harsh, brushing away
my foolishness
like irritating smoke.

AT RISK

Could there be some
subtle wisdom in whittling
down the bones, our clever bodies
sloughing excess so delicately
that we scarcely notice
our wedding rings dancing
loosely on our fingers, or
our feet gliding over carpets
light as flutes.

My doctor doesn't think so.
His voice is grim when he
warns me about osteoporosis,
the word's six syllables
marching across his tongue with
the ominous slowness of
penitents to church. Tales of
spontaneous fractures follow,
bones cracking and snapping
as the luckless
turn over in their beds.

I know the pitch, how it's
inevitable that we will lose our
bones if not our wits because
we live so long beyond our
reproductive years. My doctor
shakes his head as he reveals
the destiny of fools who turn
their threatened backs on
estrogen replacement, how

their brittle bones may splinter
from the jolt of a friendly kiss.

Though properly chastened,
I'm not yet ready to give in.
When he offers me a month's
supply of pills, the package
emblazoned with a picture of
a winged butterfly, I see
myself in flight, soaring high
above his leaden prophesies.

Calm and decorous as
Mary Poppins
(who looked rather
porously bony herself)
I'd drape my aging frame
on air, balancing
lightness and loss.

II.

CHANGELINGS

The foxes bred for tameness at the
Institute for Genetics, Novosibirsk, Siberia

The first pair, chosen
for the cooler gleam within
their yellow eyes,
shrank from human contact,
snarling and snapping if
their silver coats were touched.
By day they paced resentfully,
at night, ancestral urges
churning in their brains,
they pressed their pointed noses
towards the dark
and bit the metal fence.

Forty years and more than
forty thousand births
chart their transformation
from the wild—
these charming creatures
greeting us with waving
bushy tails and prancing feet.

But are they dogs or foxes?
Muzzles blunt, tails spiraling
above their variegated coats,
they frolic on the Institute's
wide lawn, as guileless in their
play as those enchanted animals

who lure their quarry into
tangled forests,
step by jaunty step.

IN THE ROSE TEST GARDENS, PORTLAND OREGON

These roses are being tested.
Every day the examiners come,
men in suits and women
wearing big decorated hats,
and every day the roses stumble in
drowsy and confused
to take their tests.

Hands poke them open, inspecting.
Questions are asked.
The roses don't know the answers,
so they make things up,
brazen it out with good manners
and glib responses
passing mainly on their looks.

Naturally, some fail.
Frail roses, dumb roses,
stubborn and distracted roses,
twisting their ruffled petals
and sweating hard as they
try to muddle through.
But the examiners are not fooled.

Slowly they shake their heads
and point their thumbs straight down,
flunking roses back into the dust.

DREAMING ALL OVER THE MAP

I wake at midnight in one of
New York's shabby furnished rooms
to find a bulge beneath
the covers that turns out to be
an enormous marmalade cat.
He's friendly and obviously lost.
When the super offers to find
the missing owners, I'm grateful until
I find ink on poor beast's face and
realize he's been Xeroxed.
You said you wanted posters!
shouts the super, adding that he
just spent the entire day
plastering them on every outside wall
from here to Queens. Jeez,
he was only trying to help.

And now, to make things worse,
something's scratching in
the rafters overhead. It's squirrels,
the Oregon woods are full of them,
but then I realize that it's Dr. Freud,
thoughtfully stroking his beard!
Now zhink, he says, his voice
encircling the couch, W*ho iss dis copycat?*
I try to think, but fall instead
into another dream,
the scratching sound persisting,
like a cat determined to get in.

WHEN YOU GOT TOP BILLING

for Dashka

For a moment I was one of
our peasant ancestors
guarding a piece of earth
not half the size of
our performing space.

I said: *The custom is to list
readers alphabetically.* I said:
I am the poet known to this audience.
I said: *I am her* mother.
I said: *Put me first.*

Instantly, the stars
above me lurched from their
inky tracks and plummeted,
exploding all civilized worlds.
(What kind of mother says that?)

Darling, I remember your first poem.
We lived on Barbados when
you were four, and you sang it
to the air as you dug up
sand ferociously beside
the sparkling sea. It was called

The Saddest Man in Canada..

BORROWERS

The ruling three librarians
were cloned from the same mean egg:
same thin mouths,
same impatient hands
seizing each returning book
like contraband. Methodically,
they'd sniff at spines and bindings,
fingering pages for incriminating stains.
They knew how children treated books—
those junior thugs who embellished
margins with leavings from
lunches or noses and cut photos
of naked statues from the
Encyclopedia Britannica
with hidden Exacto knives.

Browsing the children's shelves,
reading silently at the miniature tables,
writing notes on index cards
for school reports—
these were proper uses of the building,
but the scofflaws who daily
invaded their sanctum
would seldom leave it at that.
Three pairs of eyes were hardly enough
to keep track of those sneaks
burrowing into books intended
for adults, three pairs of ears
insufficient for identifying the whisperers
and showing them the door. But it was

unnecessary questions that made their
identical heads ache. Marching
some lazy culprit to the card catalogue,
they'd pull out a long oak drawer,
riffle through it with
the eraser end of a pencil
faster than our eyes could follow,
deftly pick the perfect card
like a magician retrieving
the ace of hearts, then turn
on sturdy heels with a parting shot,
"Next time, *look.*"

At five o'clock we'd line up
at the check-out desk,
where the librarian in charge
pinned back covers with her elbow
while briskly stamping due dates
within the narrow boxes
and reminding us that late fines
were a penny a day, *on every book.*
Breathing in her lurid perfume
of glue and talcum powder,
we'd solemnly nod—almost free.

Finally, books held tight against
our chests, we'd make our getaway,
racing down the wide stone steps
to the street's bright anarchy.

INCOGNITO

Ypsilanti State Hospital, 1957

I'm twenty-one, destined since
I was a mouthy kid of eight
to end up in a place like this. Back then,
I'd have been the last to guess
how easily I'd beat the wrap, but
here I am, larger in my
starched white coat, with a ring
of keys jingling at my waist—
everything legit.

Why not? In fairy tales
reversing fate depends primarily
on cleverness. With luck,
you may find helpful fishes, amulets,
potions that can change your size,
but when the chips are down and
magic is in short supply,
what's left is wit.
        (I chose a good disguise.)

I'm twenty-one, a novice
terrified by curses from this
woman more than twice my age
who screams that I'm the one
her voices warned against.
Each hour I dim inside
the brightness of my coat,
shame myself by shrinking from
the man in jungle camouflage

32

who flags me down to bellow
in a voice made hoarse by
ancient fears and nicotine,
"Those bastards took my ration book!"
He's pleading now:
Without coupons and his
tattered map, how can he buy
gasoline or groceries, how escape
the murderous yellow Japs?
I'm twenty-one, from eight till five
I'm paid to supervise these
exiles from humanity, and twice
a week explore their histories
with relatives who squirm and
fidget in their chairs as they
carefully omit details of
violence and incest. Cowed by
my white coat, they smile politely,
blinking at my questions as though
each contained a blinding light
directed at their eyes. Some ignore
the mailed appointment card,
a few send fragmented replies
in letters crudely spilled across the page:
>FBI, the sewers, no one knows,
>aliens, a dossier, fillings in my teeth,
>can't leave the house, why are you
>tormenting me?

When I put down my pen
the families leave, relieved
to hear the heavy doors
shut behind their backs. Some return
for visits, but many disappear

for months or years. And me?
I leave at five, reappear
at eight, my ring of keys
a reassuring weight.

I'm twenty-one, I don't know how
to silence the cacophony
inside these tortured minds
or tame the demons sending orders
from the radio. In fact, I'm helpless
even to prevent the evil buzzing of
fluorescent lights, erase
the smell of piss from corridors,
or quell the warning
thrumming in my bones that
soon or late they'll strip me of
my coat and keys and
claim me as their own.

MODEL MUGGERS

for Dashka

Months after finishing the course
you show me your graduation video,
a horror film in which
your co-star is the prowling beast
of nightmares who grabs you
when you least expect it,
shock silencing your screams.

On the screen I watch him
saunter into view, an outsized
Frankenstein in padded suit
and helmet. Because you know
the script, you take my hand
the way I took yours during
scary movies years ago, telling me
with the pressure of your fingers
that even though he could easily
crush the life from your slender body
the way guys at softball games
crush beer cans with one hand while
they keep on talking to a pal,
it's only a movie and everything's going
to be all right. But it's not,
because he has you on the ground
with his knee on your chest, his
obscene crotch shadowing your face
while he pins you like a butterfly,
breathing threats into your ears and eyes

and nose, every word a paralyzing poison.
His knee presses harder on your chest,
his awful *weight* as he shoves
a bulge like an exaggerated codpiece
at your mouth. You're holding my hand
very tight, my wild hand that doesn't
want to be restrained, that wants to drag
this monster off you and tear the flesh
beneath his padded suit. I'm thinking
I can't watch this, can't just sit here
on the couch—when suddenly
you become your own rescuer, exploding
from the ground like a volcano, slamming him
with a force that shakes the screen and
doesn't quit until he's down for the count.

You're standing over him, breathing hard
when you release my hand. You're there
and here, whole, unharmed—
Here! And I breathe, too.

RESCUE

They sometimes doze,
folded wings
supporting them beside
their telephones until
a sudden, jarring ring
propels them into action,
eyes merciless
as hawks' in flight.

We do not hear
their whirring wings,
nor feel their
shuddering breath before us,
never sense
a quickening of the light.
In fact, we're miffed—
>   *lottery lost*
>   *plane missed*
>   *lover ending it*
Rolling down their sleeves,
they silently
watch us weep. Too vexed
to offer comfort or advice,
they shrug their aching
shoulder blades,
unfurling opalescent wings
like silken kites.

MELODRAMA

The scene is a yellow kitchen,
yellow shining from a ceiling light
and glimmering from the walls.
As the curtain rises, a young girl enters
in a rain-soaked mackintosh.
She's laughing, but abruptly stops
as her mother, who is intently
chopping spinach, turns to
point her paring knife
at a puddle on the floor. Her face is
drained of color and her eyes stare.

The audience stirs anxiously.
What have they missed? Is this
just a little murky water or
a pool of blood? Quickly, the girl
unfurls a giant cloth, throwing herself
upon the pale linoleum to mop away
all evidence. Order is restored,

but now there is disturbance at
the stove! Seizing a long-handled
spoon and advancing with
the steely calm of a lion-tamer,
the mother turns down the flame
with her free hand,
fearlessly reaching with the spoon
to subdue a hissing pot.

Quite suddenly, a key clicks loudly
in a distant lock. What a noise!

As the audience leans forward,
tensed for the entrance of the villain,
the girl races from the room,
squealing with delight. In a moment
she returns, leading a man old enough
to be her father. In fact, that's exactly
who he is! The audience laughs with
surprised relief.—The villains
have been already vanquished:
dirty puddles, mutinous pots.

Now the stage lights dim, and music
softly heralds the final scene. While
her family watches with glistening eyes,
the mother dons mitts the yellow color
of the walls, slowly opens the oven door—
and reveals the roast! There are shouts
from her co-stars and cheers from
the audience as she moves to center stage,
raising the pan with its beautiful prize aloft.
Saluting her, father and daughter wave
gleaming knives and forks, trumpets
echo triumph, and the curtain falls
to thunderous applause.

SLEEPWALKER—2

Her smile is not her real smile,
voice not her real voice.
She does not mind this century of
vacuuming, trips to market
and drycleaner because none of it
is real. The check-out clerk's nails
clicking on rows of keys
are not real, the pungent smell
of chemicals as she collects
her cleaning no more real
than her shoes or family.
Only sleep is real.
After the false bedtime rituals,
only dreams are true.

> *Briar Rose,* calls the black dog,
> *I am your prince. Come with me.*

He is digging, his great paws
churning the earth,
clods of dirt flying like
old soft bones flung from
their burying ground, pelting
her shoulders, head, face.

And she wakes.

SNOW WHITE REMEMBERS HOW IT WAS

I tell you it was a great relief—
the end of our sinister
hide and seek. I'd had enough
of combs with savage teeth and
crimson apples hiding death
beneath their skins.

Finished! I thought as I fell,
and *Finished!* again at the funeral,
where safe within my crystal cell
I heard the Queen's exultant shriek
echo through the air.

(How foolish
everything seemed, even
the cries of my manikins,
spoiling the coffin's gleaming lid
with salty tears.)

At last, the noisy rituals were done.
The Queen's mirror confirmed
her triumph, the little men
retreated to their hearth,
and silence fell on me
like snow, nestling
white and heavy on my chest.

Beneath its weight
I lay still in my glass box,
every thought suppressed

while the earth creaked on,
issuing demands.
For one long moment I was
the only person in a world where
nothing was required of me,
not even breath.

Oh, it was too brief!
That perfect solitude I knew
before being jolted back
by his loud kiss.

III.

HORSES IN DREAMS

They are brown or gray
with shaggy winter coats. Always
they are going somewhere,
following a road or looming over
cars on city streets. Trudging
in a ragged pack,

their warm breath clouds the air,
surrounding them with vapor
like the haze designed for
flashbacks in a movie
or the science-fiction test tube
that means the end of the world.

They are tired, these horses,
so tired and uncared for,
their heaving sides revealing
the shape of an entire ribcage,
their thick and shoeless hooves
fringed with matted hair.

But where are they going
with such determination?
Trotting now, their backs quiver,
ears flatten at the skittish
evening shadows
taunting them beneath

the streetlight's glare.
Cautiously, some begin
to whinny, eyes brightening.

necks straining against
the darkness as though
they're almost there.

A DREAM MAKING MANY THINGS BETTER

My father sent flowers to my mother
the day before he died,
but they did not arrive until after
he had gone. He wished to express
his appreciation, it was as simple as that.
His illness had lasted very long.
My mother was frightened when she saw
the messenger standing in her doorway
holding a glorious bouquet. The boy
offered her the flowers, a Redon fantasy of
peonies and roses and tiny violets,
but she could not move to take them
from his hands. The doctor
had just left, she hadn't phoned
the children far way, or cried.
Who could have sent flowers so soon?

My father, when he called the florist,
could barely hold the phone
with his thin hands. It kept slipping
while he steadied it with
chin and shoulder, his breath raspy,
louder than his words: "What I want is
a big old-fashioned bouquet."
He was very weak, replacing the receiver
was hard. Soon she would come
with his pills, hold his hand, offer
water through an accordion-pleated straw.
(Did he remember to say he wanted
 baby's breath and lots of foliage?)

Closing his eyes he drifted,
dreamed of flowers in the park
when he was a boy, of flowers growing wild
in the fields near his parents' birthplace,
which he had never seen.

BELOW

In her eighty-eighth year,
when she has conquered
the illusion of time,
she rides again
with the elevator man.

The year is 1909,
and the basement with its
secret room lies so far below
the world of light
that each trip there is like
a journey to the center of the earth.

"Going down," he tells her with a wink
while she traces curlicues
on the tarnished cage,
her stomach thrilled and tight.
At the bottom they
bump, stop, bump,
and he cautions, "Watch your step,"

but she is only five—
much too young for irony,
or even to follow the song he sings
as they make their way
past a curtain
behind the furnace room.

"So hot!" she protests,
as she always does,
then holds up her arms to his

capable hands, and surrenders
her woolen dress.

How long did it last, that long
jarring ride in his clanging,
metal ship? One day
the rattling gate swung wide
and the man vanished
for eighty years. Now he holds
the key to a small, hot room
and beckons, pretending
not to notice how she's aged.

BIRTHDAY PORTRAIT IN MUTED TONES

In this expanse of pale couches
and bone-colored carpet
the artifacts refuse to age. After
years of sun and heat, they still seem
like new arrivals popped from
cardboard cartons yesterday. The light
shining through the wide windows
makes me giddy. I want to press
bowls and baskets down harder
on their tables, pound chairs
into the rug, give things weight.
My brother sits in what was
once my father's place. His hair
is gray like mine. Here
where we were never children
we rekindle old resentments over
the three-tiered cake. We are
the bad fairies at this celebration,
avenging slights. Our mother,
if she notices, gives no sign.
She smiles as we push our presents
towards her, picks intently
at the wrappings with slow-motion
hands. Reaching from my nearer seat
to help, I see how white her hair is,
bent over the stiff, bright bows.

DOCUDRAMA

From the South Side of Chicago
my mother called the North Side aunts
each week to get the news.
"How's everything?" she'd say,
and settle down for a lengthy chat
with everyone except Aunt Helen,
who always had the same resigned reply.
"Under control," was all of it,
which sounded ominous enough,
but was a flagrant lie. Aunt Helen
was married to my father's brother Joe,
a man who seemed always
in terror for his life. Eyes darting,
hands groping for a cigarette,
he visited each fear upon
Aunt Helen and Cousin Barbara,
so that their small apartment shuddered
with his dark imaginings from
the cupboards to the console radio.

For years it was the same,
then things got worse. Uncle Joe
drank more, slept less, and
finally died after an agonizing
illness that left his wife and daughter
drained beside his empty bed, their eyes
black holes of self-reproach.
Whatever they had done for him
was not enough.

Within a year they each found men
who looked enough like Uncle Joe
to be his twin. Aunt Helen married hers,
but Barbara reacted to the shock
of flesh against her flesh
by fleeing into insanity. During those
lost months all the uncles got involved,
calling the hospital, the doctors,
Aunt Helen, while electroshock
played havoc with the long and short
of memory, subdued the light within
my cousin's eyes, and waxed her skin.

At last, her demons calmed, the three
went West, where Barbara moved into
an L.A. condo prepared and paid for
by her mother and the kindly
double of her dad—
a smaller version of their own,
conveniently next door. After Helen
and her second husband died (too young),
Barbara stayed as close to home
as her recurring madness would allow.

For company she had a little dog
until the cleaning woman
carelessly allowed it to escape
(or sold it) during another
hospital stay. The loss of Alfie
made her sad life sadder,
yet everyone still hoped:
hoped each time "away"
would be the last, hoped

she'd find some friends or get
another pet, hoped for a boyfriend
who didn't look like Joe, hoped
even that she'd make some
cheerful use of Helen's
strappy shoes and linen suits.

As the last surviving aunt, my mother
still kept tabs by phone.
"How's everything?" she'd begin,
prepared to hear another eerie proof
that nothing was under control.
In a voice slurred from medications
Barbara spun elaborate tales of
strangers tampering with locks or
whispering filthy invitations
through the walls. When she died,

phones rang in several cities as
word was passed to cousins
who'd been out of touch with her
for years, all of us
more saddened than surprised.

BREATH

His chest keeps getting bigger
while the rest of him shrinks..
We meet near the edge
of his elevated mattress,
his arms reaching from
the scant blue sleeves of
summer p.j.'s, his hands
as he embraces me
delivering up too much
of his frail weight. He kisses me
(clumsily, hit-or-miss,)
and the effort turns his face
the color of dull brick.

When he was a boy with
fragile lungs, his father took him
to the gas works for a cure.
Breathe, instructed my grandfather,
and in went the penetrating fumes
like a choking death,
which proved he needed it.

Long before he was our father,
he'd switched to cigarettes.
Every New Year's Day he took
the pledge to quit, tossing us
a crackling pack of Chesterfields
to get rid of as we wished. (Usually
we ripped the paper casings off,
then trampled them to smithereens
beneath our rubber boots.)

These days his beetle chest
resembles that bulky pack of
Lucky Strikes that used to dance
across the TV screen on
jaunty legs—except that his
thin shanks can barely make it
from his wheelchair to the bed.
Propped against pillows,
he speaks, wheezes, signals
with his hand for me to wait.

I wait, my own chest tight
in air that now feels thinner,
while he captures
the next elusive breath.

FINALLY

She's free now, no more
crazy mother to take care of
and no more whiney kids and no more
husband wheezing ever more slowly
over twenty years. She's free
to read the Sunday Times
with no one interrupting, to leave
her bed at night solely for her own
bladder's sake, to learn Italian,
plan a trip, buy marmalade
for her solitary toast.

IMPRINT

What if she'd been famous and
much photographed—an adorable
Shirley Temple or Natalie Wood?
In the only newspaper snapshot
(fuzzy reprint of one taken with
a two-buck Brownie camera)
she was just a pudgy six year old with
short blonde hair. Back then,

there was no CNN to flash
the news every fifteen minutes,
no raging father fashioning a career
out of some cop's carelessness,
not even features in the Enquirer
about her final days. I can't remember
any pictures of her grieving parents,
just that blurry thumbnail shot of
blonde Suzanne,
her smile slightly grimacing
because the sun was in her eyes.

Imagine an announcer's voice
abruptly cutting off
the Lux Radio Theater to report
that the missing child's head
had been discovered in a sewer,
the words so startling that parents
couldn't turn the switch
in time to save their children
from the blaring radio.

Which actually made no difference.

The truth was out:
parents were frauds if someone
could run a ladder up to
a little girl's bedroom
and abduct her from her bed.

Only weeks after that initial horror
his lipsticked scrawl turned up
on another victim's mirror:
"Stop me before I kill more
I cannot control myself,"

> *Stop that giggling,*
> *Stop teasing your sister,*
> *Stop that crying or I'll give you*
> *something to cry about.*

And we couldn't,
we couldn't no matter what.

Suzanne Degnan's death
changed everything. From that day on
we knew that terrible things could happen
to us, and that parents who made rules and
spanked and took away allowances
were useless when the chips were down,
when someone was *really* out of control.

The worst part was her being
so ordinary, a girl who squinted
just when the shutter clicked
and was kind of fat. For years
I was haunted by the memory
of her face and his—a boy from
the University of Chicago

who didn't look crazy or evil
in the newspaper pictures,
a nice-looking boy with dark hair and
a pleasant smile who'd slipped
through a gate one moonless night

and couldn't stop.

HOUSE ARREST

For Kaspar Hauser in an earlier time,
the girl known as Genie in ours,
and the many whose stories are not known.

Imprisoned for years in
darkened rooms, they play with
a secret scrap of bone,
dressing it in bits of cloth,
then stripping it bare again.
Finally, when the hidden door
is found, they limp crookedly
to safety on the arms of
rescuers whose urgent speech
they cannot understand.

Not really children, they'll never
be adults, although in time
they may recite a few
misshapen words or
eat with spoons. Free to
navigate a world transformed
by sun and air,
they're captive still,

alarmed by human touch,
confused by light.

MY GRANDMOTHER'S EDUCATION

Sharlotta was smart enough,
the convent was not too far,
and the nuns would
teach her to read. Imagine it,
this scared Jewish child
sitting stiffly on a bench,
unable to follow the prayers.
At supper she heard
her classmates whisper how
they'd seen the points of horns
protruding from beneath
her braided hair. Secretly

she felt her suspect forehead,
homesickness ticking
in her throat, until the day
when words flew up like butterflies
before her eyes, arriving
like magicians on her slate.
It *was* magic,
this silken opening of doors
where no doors were,
this gliding over thresholds
into rooms shimmering with light.
It didn't matter any more
that girls slid over
on the bench so their elbows
wouldn't touch—her discovery was
company enough. Each morning

she woke remembering the graceful way
words sidled from one page of
her primer to the next.

Then one night a fever crept
beneath the quilt, wrapping her
in scarlet flames and smoking out
the nimbused butterflies. Afterwards,
there were only ashes left.
The whitewashed convent walls
seemed ominous, the convent food
went uneaten on her plate.
She opened books
to stare at a's and b's and c's,
those crippled acrobats,
but none of their tricks made sense.

Eventually, the nuns inspected
her copybook. They could
no longer keep her,
a disappointing pupil with
so much leakage in her head,
but the novices were kind when
they helped her pack. Halfway home,
Sharlotta gasped. Searching
bags and bundles she found that
it was true—she'd left
her useless primer behind
the convent gates,
and there was no going back.

That was the end of it.
At her father's table
the littler children leaned to see

her careful manners, and in
the sewing room her mother
called back seams and fancy work
from their forgotten place.
After awhile no one spoke
of her time away, or guessed that
in her bed at night
she conjured books and pencils
while threads of moonlight
inched their way along the walls,
like fingers
looking for a door.

LEGACY

Goodbye Sharlotta
gold is running in the streets
send for you when I can
kiss the kids.

Is that what he said in his note,
my mother's handsome father,
when he left my grandmother in Hungary
to wait for him?
Well, something of the sort.

If my other grandfather
had attempted such a trick
my Grandmother Sarah would have
gone after him in the wagon
and brought him home,
the way she did when they took him
for the Polish Infantry.

But my Grandmother Sharlotta
drew her four children
closer to her knees and waited,
grateful that three of them were boys.
For ten years
relatives brought her groceries
by cover of night to save her shame,
and a borrowed servant
still called her *gnadige fraü.*
When the littlest boy died
a relative wrote the sad news
to the husband in America,

since a fever in her girlhood
took with it most of what
Sharlotta learned in school.

Fever or no fever,
my Grandmother Sarah
would have written the letter in blood
and swum it herself
across the cold Atlantic,
demanding blood for blood.

But my Grandmother Sharlotta
packed up her three surviving children
when the boat fare came,
and joined her handsome husband
in New York. This is where
we find them, in a modest
fourth floor walkup where
he's given her another baby
for a fortieth birthday gift.
He doesn't seem to like her
any better than before,
but he comes home every night
(often late), and forgives her
many failings—confusion,
helplessness, impatience with
the new little girl.
Her brain is weak, he sighs,
recalling the fever of her youth.
Sharlotta silently bites her lip,
but I make a different choice,

You did this, I tell him,
in my Grandmother Sarah's voice.

POINTS OF VIEW

There were hundreds of them!
I tell her, *Hundred of wild swans*
filling the air above my head like an
exploded feather quilt! I want to say more,
tell her how weightlessly they glided
through their bright confetti sky,
describe the way they called to one another
with loud cacophonous delight,
but I don't get the chance. Drawing
her cardigan closer, my mother
sits forward in her chair and warns,
Those are very dangerous birds.

MAGICIANS

Because she worshiped
new inventions, I like to show
my dead mother
how my computer works.
"This is cut and paste," I say,
cool and efficient as those
gray-suited guides in the
Science Museum
who showed us human innards
and dial phones
and took our fifth grade class
on a jolting elevator ride
to a model coal mine
miles below
the rotunda's marble floor—
a place something like the scene
of Pinnochio's come-uppance.

In the dim catacomb,
they leaned close
to calm our claustrophobic fears,
but showing my mother
how to mark a paragraph for doom,
I'm as cocky as my brother John,
who once removed the tarnish
from his heavy I.D. bracelet
by lowering it from a string
into a crock of cyanide
in the basement of our father's
jewelry shop.

I remember the smell of
bitter almonds
as he pulled it from the poison
like a gleaming silver fish.
Deadpan behind his metal
eye-glass frames
(the bracelet curled and
shining in the sink),
he solemnly explained
that a single drop of
what was in that crock
was enough to kill a horse.

Seated at my elbow,
my mother is
the perfect audience.
While the words I'm writing
still merit no response,
the way I bend the
computer's will to mine
inspires the little snort
that tells me she's impressed.
As I show how neatly
my files within files are arranged,
she shakes her head
in wonder, the way she did
when my brother
(who is also dead)
mixed up our first reconstituted
frozen orange juice,
and poured
the gorgeous liquid
into a tall, clear glass.

IV.

FIRST LOVE

There once was a girl who loved a horse.
There were hundreds of this girl,
there were thousands. She thought
all the time about her horse, the one that
she alone knew. She drew pictures of
her horse in the margins of her notebook,
she wrote his name again and again,
she called him Carthage, she called him
Lancelot, she called him Fireweed.
She wrote stories about him and poems
about him, and at night she dreamed of
herself and him, galloping sometimes,
sometimes flying, her eager voice
urging him, singing his name, her body
hugging his like the lover she was,
the perfect lover of her magic horse,
her horse, hers.

EROTICA

Maybe it was her heaviness and silence
or her parochial school uniform
or the book he once grabbed
from her hands called
A Child's Lives of the Saints.
Whatever the source, it was
classic lust, though my brother insisted
that he hated Margaret Sullivan,
whose rose-papered bedroom
in the building next door
was directly opposite his.

In the late afternoon he'd watch
for her, this stolid dark-haired girl
with squarish hips. I can picture her
turning the corner of our street
at four o'clock, eyes focused on
the sidewalk, her body stiff with fear
that this awful boy, a whole year
younger than herself,
might be lurking somewhere,
ready to soil her with a look.

He did that a lot, staring with
an insinuating sneer or
smirking to himself. Still,
Margaret never guessed
what he was up to
the day he stooped to tie his shoe
just as she approached.
Stepping carefully around him,

her armload of books held tight
against her chest, she was only steps
from the safety of her door when
he sprang up noisily beside her,
shouting for all the world to hear
that there was a hole the size of Texas
in Margaret Sullivan's underwear.

Within minutes our mother got a call
from Mrs. Sullivan, and my brother
was grounded for a week,
a penance he spent mostly
behind his bedroom door.
"What do you suppose she prays about?"
he asked me near the end of his
long punishment, his eyes
so bright with excitement that
any fool could tell
he believed she was praying for him.

RESUMÉ

When her life seemed
too demanding,
my mother often claimed
it was her sole ambition
to stand in some monotonous
factory line, watching cans
of beans roll by. She wouldn't
mind the pay because
her simple job would be to
drop a piece of pork
on top of each. On better days
she craved a business of her own,
some classy place with
her name on the awning that
she ruled in a good gray suit.

Now the direction of her gaze
has changed. She focuses on what
she hasn't been— a faster reader,
better shopper, thin. As she recites
her litany of disappointment,
I see her in that scheme she once
imagined: A conveyer belt
is humming, and a thousand cans
are floating by like objects in a dream.
Beneath the cool fluorescent lights
my mother lifts her hand, a girl
with a paycheck coming,
and nothing but
this moment on her mind.

JULY

for Dashka

In the pool a young woman
floats on her back in a brilliant
turquoise suit, her hands
treading water just
enough to buoy her up.
With her eyes closed
she knows she fills the pool,
length and breadth, imagines
other bathers pressed tight
against the edge as her belly
crowns the water royally.
It is a splendid shiny being,
this belly, with its own
mysterious sea and
a swimmer who also stirs
the water and kicks its feet.

Mirrors within mirrors,
thinks the woman in the pool,
the inside of her eyelids splashed
with sunlight, her breathing
synchronized
with underwater messages
lapping at her heart. Now
ripples break the water's
gentle shimmer as her belly
rises higher and she sighs into
another perfect moment.
Everything blue and bright.

ACQUIRED TASTE

for Elizabeth

It's greed that makes me furtive.
I'm here as an invited guest,
urged to fill my paper sack from
rows of chard and broccoli.
Still, I feel like a thief,
like Rapunzel's frantic mother,
so possessed by her craving
for rampion that she clawed
the black earth
like a dog tearing its way
to a ripened bone,
not caring that the price of
this shameful passion
was her only beloved child.

What would my mother think,
remembering our endless
vegetable wars, to see me
wolfishly pulling carrots
from their beds? Maybe this is
a normal turnabout, maybe
even Rapunzel's mother
once swung her legs beneath
a rough wood table,
refusing her beautiful greens.

THE SEAMSTRESS'S ASSISTANT

Thread binds me to her.
Her ghostly shape is in
this slippery silk,
her spine's small notches
curl beneath the hundred
buttons of her gown.
(Does she fidget in her sleep
as I smooth the placket down?)

In these murky hours
I keep myself alert
imagining some small mistake.
Tonight I'm thinking of a pin,
tucked like a curse between
embroidered flowers and ruching,
ready for mischief
when the waltz begins.

> *Oh, the blueness of her eyes*
> *as she abruptly halts,*
> *at first more mortified than pained.*
> *Her puzzled smile slides down*
> *her chin like wax beneath*
> *a candle flame. And look!*
> *A crimson stain is spreading*
> *on the ivory silk. (A pity after*
> *so much costly work.)*

Silk rustles in my lap as
as I finish up the hem—my little
circle dance. You'd think

this work would make my fingers
thick as sausages, but seeing them
in the lamplight as I stitch
they seem pathetic, each one
skinny as the bone that
Gretel used to fool the witch.

DREAM OF AN X-RATED MOVIE

A young man with thick dark hair
and his frail distracted mother
lie wrapped in each other's arms
on a rosy satin comforter,
his naked body covering
the confusion of her white flesh
and white disheveled nightgown,
four pearl buttons open
at the throat. The camera follows
her fluttering hands as
a narrator's voice explains
> *It was the only way*
> *to save her from*
> *the taxi driver, gardener,*
> *the drifter's deadly smile.*

Suddenly the angle veers from
hands to thrusting hips, the
mother's body arcing upwards as
her mouth records a silent no.
The camera moves in for a close-up
shot through a grainy lens:
First, the pearl buttons,
shining like tears, then
the boy's smooth back as
the narrator's voice exclaims,
> *Must every son demand*
> *the underside of love!*

The camera rests on the
young man's face as he gasps

and sighs. It's all over,
yet we stay with that face,
younger now within its frame of
damply curling hair. Still
pinned beneath him, his mother
melts into the satin quilt,
one translucent hand
fastening the buttons at her throat.

EROS

He loves costumes,
the flowers pinned all over
his black suit. At night
in the darkened theater
he sews builds sets adapts
the script, in the morning
posts announcements
in elaborate calligraphy,
disappearing ink.

WOMAN, TREE, BOYS

Look, there is a woman
sitting on the branch of
that tree. She is not a bird
but she sings, not a cat
but she howls and shrieks and
scrapes her nails across
the bark. Now her voice goes
deadly calm as she reports
the evening news to no one
in particular, ignoring the boys
shimmying up the trunk
to see what's what. There are
three of them, showing off for their
pals below, bringing their faces
close to hers, beating their chests.
Probably they are thoroughly scared
by what they've done, seen,
guessed, but you'd never know it
from their Tarzan cries or
the jaunty way they bounce among
the leaves. "Crackpot!" they shout,
pitching acorns at her branch.
  Why is she so stubborn?
  Why can't they make her flinch?

ZINNIAS

for John

1.
They're not my favorites,
but they were his. Brilliant as he was,
he didn't know much about gardening,
and never bothered to find out.
He just loved zinnias—brazen colors,
lusty blooms. Every year
he drove a hundred baby plants to
the windy beach house, checking
the car's back seat at stop lights
to make sure they were still all right.

"I've got *Cut and Come Again*,"
he phoned to tell me once,
miles ahead of all the jerks who
fell for the fleeting, gaudy promises
of Zenith or State Fair. Another time
he planted zinnias in a sun-scorched
patch of desert, filling the entire
strip of Arizona earth
that edged our mother's patio.

Near the end I brought zinnias
to the hospital, big jazzy flowers
radiating hope. Opening his eyes,
he looked at the madcap blossoms
cheering from their vase and
gave a brief indifferent nod that
stopped whatever words

I might have said.

2.
A year later I cut an armload of
scarlet and magenta zinnias
for his first memorial bouquet,
remembering too late that I'd
just been trimming herbs and
the scissors in my hand was
releasing essence of cilantro
at every snip. Cilantro!
which he hated so intensely
that once in an Indian restaurant
he made the whole rowdy table of us
surrender half the condiments
before permitting us to eat.

John will be furious! I thought,
feeling dumb and guilty until
a friend attempting contact with
the other side relayed a message
meant for me: "Please give
my good wishes to my sister,"
she read from a scrap of paper
in a voice that was nothing like his.

What was I supposed to make of it?
For weeks I repeated this oddly
formal greeting to myself,
the words taking on the unlikely
brilliance of flowers blooming
in the dead of winter,

and the thought of cilantro

polluting his zinnias
becoming the kind of silliness
I knew he would have liked.

V.

ABRIDGED NOVEL WITH PREDICTABLE OUTCOME

For years you strive for recognition,
demonstrating worth and versatility like
a kitchen gadget in an expert
pitchman's hands. You'll try anything:
high-wire walker, complaints clerk, translator
of forgotten tongues. Then, when hope is all but
exhausted, you click—an overnight success!
The kitchen gadget does a tap dance
on its own steam, the high-wire widens
to a boulevard, everyone speaks your language,
and there are absolutely no complaints.
You buy new clothes, a shiny car, get invited
everywhere. Each time you sell your memoirs
it's a different tale. During interviews
you lift your skirt, show *Born to Win*
tattooed in colors on your thigh. Now
the phone rings day and night—new friends,
departed lovers, your entire high school class.
They call you by old nicknames, laugh at
pranks you don't remember, (a few claim
unpaid debts). You buy a private plane,
a country home, hire a cook and bodyguard,
unlist your phone. Over a solitary
Scotch and soda, you recall the years
of struggle, fantastic events that happened
to someone else. Outside your sleek glass house
the applause continues, ominous as drums.

RESTRICTIONS

Even though it was cold and
one of them had to pee,
my brother's enemies waited
patiently. Finally,
when the super had finished
patching up our tilted yard
with fresh cement, they rose from
their huddle on the steps and
wrote beneath the basketball hoop
with a sharpened stick :
> *This Court is Restricted*
> *to John Appel.*

Then they watched their message
harden into law, clapped each other
on the back, and scampered off,
vanishing behind doors identical
to ours. At last, they'd found a way
to whip my brother's ass.

Or so they thought. John
said he now was guaranteed
exclusive rights to everything:
communal hoop and backboard,
patched cement, a row of dank
unused garages, and that narrow strip
of earth next to the fence,
glittering with shards of broken glass.

For a week they took turns at
pushing him off the court while he

pushed back, but even when
a truce was struck, no one
bought my brother's tricky logic.
"Restricted" had a meaning
we all knew. If it worked for the
South Shore Country Club
besides entire neighborhoods
who didn't want to rent to Jews,
why couldn't Jewish boys with
gripes against a mouthy kid
restrict him?

Years later, there were scores of
others—his wife's insulted relatives,
waiters who hovered too often or
too near. (And yes, those muscle-shirted
guys in Central Park who were
too surprised to jump him when
he switched their boom box off.)
Dozens would have gladly used some
wet cement to weight his shoes,
if they couldn't just
restrict him from New York.

After his death I revisited our street,
less welcomed by its current tenants
than if, all those years before,
I'd tried to crash the restricted
Country Club. Past floodlights
hung like moons above
the narrow walkway and a
chain link gate, I was stunned
to find the shabby yard wrapped in
new concrete. Watched by

stone-faced kids lounging
on the steps, I inspected it
inch by inch, imagining that I could
simply peel it back to find
the words that shut my brother out
or made him king. As I was leaving
the kids perked up, a chorus yelling,
"Shut that gate!"

GOLDFISH

Here she is beautiful and safe.
This globe is small enough to
swim in seconds, large enough for
her to swish her wide translucent

wonder of a tail. Blowing bubbles,
she trips like a queen through
the seven turrets of her castle,
rises *en pointe* to nibble lunch.

True, it's a public life. It took
a while to learn to live without
embarrassment, to swim and
sulk and shit. Now it's simply

the nature of the world,
even the weekly airlifts to limbo
while the bowl is cleaned.
It takes about ten minutes

to make it perfect as it was
on the fifth day of creation,
when God gave the glass a final polish
and sat down to have a smoke.

MY MOTHER'S EYESIGHT

The lights do not go out at once.
First there is the long groping dusk
that can last for years,
muting colors, narrowing the view.
Now it takes something with
the verve and flash of
a parrot's wing to catch her eye.

The long pathway to the night
is lined with obstacles—leafy shapes
that dance and waver at her feet.
She squints, testing distance with
a careful step, and sometimes,
looking out the car's wide window
at the boulevard, she'll ask,
"Are we in the underpass?"

Only the window to the past is clear.
Through it she sees herself
at twenty-two, greeting my father in
her parents' entryway. As she takes
his coat and muffler,
still flecked with February snow,
an image forms behind her eyes,
enduring as a photograph:
       His hands and hers,
       meeting over cloth.

HISTORICAL ROMANCE

The final pages of this paperback
are missing, which means
I'll never know if this silly girl,
whose cloying indecision
I've put up with for
thirty seven chapters,
chooses with her heart or head.

I throw the book across the floor
and the remains of my cold coffee
down the drain, hoping that
she ditches both these wimpy guys
and grabs the first boat to Australia.
There she can find her
long-lost older brother,
shipped off years ago in chains,
who now owns fifty thousand acres
and as many sheep.

What brother?
There's been no mention of a brother.

But there could be one,
a wiry, crafty sort of man
who would applaud
her spunky break for freedom
while they swap stories
by flickering lamplight,
both of them thrilled and drunk.
This is *home*, this untamed place
where her brother's tales

97

of deals and swindles send her
into wild, malicious laughter
that shakes her coiled hair
loose from its hundred pins.

In the morning things may change.
Then she may long for England,
slap the leering ranch hand
who dares to make a pass—
or discover that this man is not
her long-lost brother, after all.

But tonight she lifts her glass and
toasts adventure: "Here's to never
knowing any outcome!" she cries,
her skirts hiked up above
her boot tops, her voice merging
with the distant sound of
sheep moving against sheep.

NO PERMANENT ADDRESS

These children fall asleep
at school but do not dream.
Awake they think of food.
Waiting with their mothers
in those dingy anterooms
where the lines stretch out
beyond the future
and move by baby steps,
they whine and fidget
on the scarred wooden benches,
hamburgers big as cows
bellowing in their heads.

THE ROSENBERGS

They got no sympathy
from my parents, those ingrates
who betrayed their country
and shamed the Jews.
And for what? To make us
Communist slaves without
cars or radios? Europe—
you could keep it! Drunken Cossacks
raping women, spitting in your face!
Why would anyone go back there
if they had a choice? For us,
a vacation was two weeks at Elkhart Lake,
except for the summer of
our famous California tour,
which brought a whole new world—
suntanned, smiling people,
sightings of movie stars, and once,
stopped at a traffic light on Sunset,
a Mexican woman with a baby
yanked open the unlocked door,
pointed at our license plates and cried,
"Take me with you, please señor!"
That trip you'd remember
all your life! The Rosenbergs
could have learned a thing or two.

TEENIES

They were miniatures,
like the celluloid pair in
my mother's drawer, saved
from her wedding cake.
Doll-sized and smiling,
you could picture them
posed on the uppermost tier—
Uncle Johnny in
glossy shoes and tux,
Aunt Bea's flaxen curls
circled by a coronet
of columbine and
baby's breath.

Once or twice a year they
whirled into our midst,
a Yorkshire Terrier
prancing at their feet. Smaller
than all but the youngest,
they basked in our meager
spotlight, bestowing smiles and
gifts like Oriental kings.

Of course, there was more
to the story: She was
a mean drunk and his
shady business dealings
forced them to live
in Canada to escape
the IRS. But Uncle Johnny
was the family hero,

a pint-sized desperado
smuggling money
across the border for
a hundred family needs,
and probably risking
jail to visit us.

To topple them feels
treasonous. Bea's nightly
descent into violence
(the Yorkie quaking
on its pillow), and those
mysterious long distance
phone calls which my father
would never discuss,

those things belong
to Canada. In my mind
they still rule brightly,
rushing to greet us with
arms outstretched,
the Yorkie
on its silken leash
keeping pace with
their tiny steps.

TIME ZONES

Chicago

I was raised to think that
old meant all things cracked,
bent, foreign, or out-of date.
It was the chip in the kitchen sink
or last year's dress. My grandparents
were old, shrunken with
the shame of it, and marked,
(their faces blotched with
umber spots like tea stains
on a tablecloth.) Sealed within
small, overheated rooms,
they kept their curtains drawn
against the city's sleight of hand:
the streets ablaze with neon,
familiar buildings gone.

Boston

It was like being in a foreign country,
this labyrinth of antique streets
ferociously preserved. On both sides of
the Charles, buildings stood on
rock unmoved for centuries,
while the elegant Back Bay,
balanced on a salt marsh,
floated blithely on. In those first
September days I traced a hodgepodge
tangle of streets and alleyways,
leading finally to Beacon Hill's
brick sidewalks, where people old as

my sequestered grandparents
promenaded slowly, wearing years
like layers of rich shawls.

BURYING MY MOTHER

1.
Her ashes have been
six months in my living room.
It's like gestation except
she will not grow, will not
be born, will stay in that gray
cardboard box underneath
the pearwood table which is
longer than a coffin and
older than this stubborn woman
who was my mother,
until I decide what to do.

The point is, she didn't decide.
Forget that for twenty years
she typed and retyped
revised editions of
"Instructions To Be Followed
Following My Death,"
each time dispatching fuzzy carbons
to my brother and myself.

My brother, another stubborn one!
And since he exited more than
a year before her, what help
could he provide? Properly buried
in a Jewish cemetery,
his bones white and clean
as driftwood on a beach,
he was silent on the subject of
paragraphs five and six.

2.
She was our mother! How could I
send her naked to the flames
or let them extract her teeth?
I read what they do in crematoriums,
she insisted more than once,
The workers go after the gold!
Where did she read that?
Was it really about practices
in Phoenix, Arizona, or was it
a description of Auschwitz?
(And how much gold
could there possibly be
in this little woman's teeth?)

Accepting the cardboard box
neatly fitted with a handle,
I was astonished by its weight.
Despite my sneaky addition
of a dress and underthings,
I'd expected her ashes to be
as light as those bits of fluff
that catch on window screens.

Halfway home, with
airplane engines droning
and the box tucked
safely overhead,
I read her final orders
one last time, line by
fuzzy carbon line.

3.
Under the pearwood table,
the box of ashes takes up
little space. Relinquishing
a lifetime of opinions,
my mother has become
an unassuming guest
whose presence I forget
for weeks and weeks.

STAIR TALK

Since neither one spoke
French, I don't know where
my parents found the idiom,
l'esprit d'escalier,
which translates more or less
as "stair talk", and means
the snappy comeback that
pops into your head
too late to pass your lips.

Once I heard a stand-up comic
quote his father's
final words at the end of
a long argument:
"It's all right, Sonny," he said,
"I'll forget and you'll forget—
but I'll remember!"

That was my family to a T,
a bunch of thin-skinned
stair-talkers, finding
the perfect answer to
an insult while mounting
the steps to bed. (For us
stair talk was also
the words we staggered
down the steps with in
the morning, and invited
to breakfast and lunch.)

From time to time
I find myself chewing
over one of my
undelivered gems, the way
I drag old poems from
tattered notebooks, trying
to get them right.
But mostly, I call back
snips of conversation
just to listen. Climbing

the stairs to my bedroom,
I talk amiably with ghosts,
announcing some new
wrinkle in the world or
in my life. The last word,
not by choice.

PASSAGE

We were like marathon dancers
on the twenty-third day or
prisoners forced to march. I was
seventeen and he was old enough
to be my father, a tall man
in a light summer suit
who suddenly slumped against
the tunnel's tiled wall,
just below the scarred mosaic
spelling out Randolph Street.

I wasn't sure he heard me
when I offered help, his eyes closed,
breath coming hard, my own voice
lost in the rush hour roar. Then
his arm was tight around
my neck, his whiskey breath
hot on my face and throat,
and we were slow-dancing towards
the station's harsh fluorescent lights,
a sweating man and a girl
supporting his shuffling weight
against her thin blue dress.

When he finally slid unconscious
to the ground, his body draped across
my sandaled foot, I didn't move.
Could I just leave him there,
this gray-haired man
who wasn't having a heart attack
after all? We were still joined

chest to foot when two young cops
pushed me gently towards my train,
then slung the man's limp arms
around their shoulders
with an easygoing heave-ho.

For weeks afterwards I felt
his heat and weight still clinging
to me when I demonstrated our
lurching zig-zag for my friends,
a wild burlesque
that made everybody laugh.
With each performance
I moved a little further from
that foolish girl
in the tunnel, till I could
scarcely remember her face.

Dori Appel's poetry has been featured in many journals, magazines, and anthologies, including six collections published by Papier Mache Press. Among these are *When I Am an Old Woman I Shall Wear Purple* and *The Best Is Yet To Be*, the audio recording of which was a 1997 Grammy finalist. A playwright as well as a poet, her work has been widely produced throughout the United States, as well as internationally. Her monologues are featured in several anthologies, and three full length plays are published by Samuel French. Working between the two genres, her poems sometimes become monologues or scenes in dramatic works. The recipient of several regional and national playwriting awards, she was the winner of the prestigious Oregon Book Award in Drama in 1998 for *Freud's Girls*, in 1999 for *The Lunatic Within*, and in 2001 for *Lost and Found*. To learn more about her poetry and plays, visit her website at http://www.doriappel.com.

Printed in the United States
214062BV00002B/3/P